Redesigning Leadership

SIMPLICITY: DESIGN, TECHNOLOGY, BUSINESS, LIFE
John Maeda, Editor

Redesigning Leadership

John Maeda

with Becky Bermont

The MIT Press
Cambridge, Massachusetts
London, England

For information about special quantity discounts, please email special_sales@ mitpress.mit.edu

This book was set in MercuryG2, Gotham, and DotMatrix by the MIT Press. Printed and bound in the United States of America.

Library of Congress Cataloging-in-Publication Data

Maeda, John.

 Redesigning leadership / John Maeda with Becky Bermont.

   p. cm. — (Simplicity: design, technology, business, life)

 Includes index.

ISBN 978-0-262-01588-2 (hardcover : alk. paper) 1. Leadership I. Bermont, Becky. II. Title. III. Series.

HM1261.M34 2011

658.4'092—dc22

                                    2010046316

10   9   8   7   6   5   4   3   2   1

"Blast away at it! Get it done!"

—*William J. Mitchell, 1944–2010*

Contents

SIMPLICITY

↓

raison d'être

Introduction

We didn't know it when I started working for him, but my partnership with John began with our professional interests set to collide. A lifetime academic who had always engaged with industry from the outside, he had just finished an MBA and was curious about what the work of leading large organizations was like. I'd finished my MBA at Stanford and, as the story often goes, had become quickly disenchanted with my immediate post-MBA job. I'd had two years at school being indoctrinated in how I could "change lives, change organizations, and change the world," and had trouble translating that to the reality of working in the middle of a big company. I wasn't sure what was wrong, but I knew that a job at the MIT Media Lab sounded sufficiently exotic that I was intrigued. It didn't hurt that I had always lived in the high tech world of Cambridge and the Bay Area, in the shadow of the lab's legend and mystique.

As we did our work together connecting the Media Lab's sponsoring companies to its research, it quickly became clear that John and I shared an almost limitless interest in introspection and in pulling out what we were learning—about ourselves, about the world—from our working experiences. When John got the opportunity to assume the helm at RISD, I couldn't resist the chance to come along. There we quickly found fertile ground for an ongoing conversation about what it means to lead in this day and age.

Perhaps not coincidentally, the transition described in this book took place at the same time that another young, inexperienced, former professor and leader of color found himself taking office as the president of the United States. Often I could see a thin thread connecting the events affecting President Obama and those that President Maeda was experiencing—the good and the bad. I took ongoing comfort in the realization that Obama was there to help our generation figure it out.

John and I have very different minds and ways of working. He draws to make sense of things; I take notes. He is constantly inventing; I am constantly organizing. He is four steps ahead and I am focused on the here and now. He takes risks and I am more worried about how things will be perceived. When we started this project, I began as I always do—by creating a logical narrative outline and a schedule. John started by designing the cover and mocking up the design of the book with dummy text, so he could get a sense of what the final product would feel like.

So I've become immersed in the brain of a creative and a coder, and he's been able to see the world through my eyes, which take on the hue of a social scientist. Most of all, though,

John's unique viewpoint has taught me the enormous value of the freedom to try, and of being unafraid to fail. The four words that underlie his simplicity book series, "Design, Technology, Business, Life," in many ways embody the productive tensions and questions that encompass our similarities and differences, and the work that we do together.

Shortly after arriving at RISD, John was quickly recognized among his college president peers as "the president who tweets." Since I run RISD's Media group, people mistakenly surmised that I was ghost-tweeting on his behalf—it's really him, and completely uncensored. His tweeting began innocently; as John says later on in this book, he sees new technological tools as "shiny objects [from which] it's impossible to turn away." Along the way, when people would ask if he was still doing his own creative work, I noticed he started to answer them by calling the tweets his "art." After a while I saw what he meant, as he used the tweets to help crystallize the lessons of the extraordinarily intense experience of "suddenly" becoming president of an institution during the worst financial crisis in decades.

So this book was created starting there—by sorting through 1,200 140-character posts; each a little haiku about redesigning leadership, or at the minimum, just coming to terms with it. John's tweets now act as the headers throughout this book. The broader experiences and insights that they brought out are certainly relevant for me, someone who is in her thirties, trying to figure out what kind of leader I want to be and realizing that how I lead can reflect the changing world that our generation is inheriting. I hope that they also resonate with John's now nearly one hundred thousand other Twitter "followers" out there, wherever they are. I've been inspired in the work I get to do with John and hope that, through this book, some of that inspiration and hope can be passed on to you.

Becky Bermont

上には上がある。

1

Start Here

There is a simple saying in Japanese that epitomizes the nature of striving for excellence, *"Ue ni wa ue ga aru."* It translates literally as, "Above up, there is something even higher above up." To me, it is an eloquent expression of not only an unattainable goal in life, but also the nature of human ambition—of constantly wanting to become better.

Becoming better can take many forms. It is easy to take matters into your own hands when it comes to improving skills like drawing, public speaking, or anything else where practice makes perfect. Advancing your own career, however, is something that is subject to an entirely different set of forces, fraught with politics, relationships, and chance, not all of which are as easily controlled.

In my own working life, questions of career advancement had largely been resolved. I had worked my way up to being a tenured professor at MIT, which is a job that I could have kept until I croaked. Sure, there were a few times during my career as a junior professor when I tried to rock the boat and I was warned, "Cool your jets, and wait in line for your turn." On another occasion, I was informed that my quest for change was pointless: "John, just wait until they all die," I was told. I took that as advice to live into my 100s, so I began exercising more and eating better to maximize my chances of making a difference. Little did I know what was about to happen long before I was 100 ...

SIMPLICITY TO COMPLEXITY

> Staring at a missing piece in your life makes you miss the real peace that you truly have.

During my career as a professor, I had begun working outside of academia with a variety of clients, either with companies as a designer, or with galleries as an artist. In doing so it became clear that there was a missing piece to my education. People kept saying to me, "You're the creative person, John, so don't worry about the financial stuff." As a professor, I had always operated my own "organization of one," but a brief stint as an administrator exposed my sheer lack of knowledge of how an organization of more-than-one is run. So I sought to remedy this deficiency with an MBA—perhaps it was the missing piece in my life that would solve all my problems. Alas, getting it made me reflect on all the amazing changes in business, technology, and design that had led to intense complexity in our daily lives. I realized that I wasn't just missing a degree, I was missing a sense of simplicity. And so I began a project to define the *The Laws of Simplicity*, which gave me the peace I was looking for ... for that moment.

> @johnmaeda is thinking how courage is a noble form of stupidity that aids getting impossible things done.

Shortly after completing *The Laws of Simplicity* and giving a related talk at the TED (Technology, Entertainment, Design) conference, I received a phone call from a headhunter about the possibility of leading a major art and design institution. I was happy to suggest names of other people the recruiter could contact instead of me, since I didn't see myself as presidential material at the time. I hadn't been a department head, dean, or provost at MIT, so I figured I should just "wait in line" as I'd been told. But the conversations continued, and before I knew it I was suddenly the sixteenth president of the Rhode Island School of Design (RISD). The fact that I "suddenly" became president continues to frame my experience even today, as I believe that not having learned all of the proper administrative ropes along the way has given me a kind of freedom and courage to improvise as needed.

"THE MAN"'S LIFE IS COMPLEX

> The grass is always greener on the other side because from
  far away you can't see the weeds.

I've quickly come to realize that being a professor/thought leader is different than being a CEO/organizational leader. There are similarities of course—being either requires a great deal of discipline and hard work. But there's much greater latitude as a professor, when you work within the ethos of academic freedom and are free to speak your mind unreservedly against "the man." The leader of an institution, on the other hand, manages infinitely more constraints with regard to what he can say. I'm embarrassed to admit that I never truly realized that the position at the top—something of aspirational value and numerous upsides—carried significant constraints. As an academic trained to speak his mind—and even worse as an artist and designer who lives to express himself creatively—it has been an interesting challenge to learn, through much trial and error, how to live as a creative leader of an institution.

> @johnmaeda is tickled by barber's response to my Q, "Do you believe in leadership by example?" "Sure. But not if it's a bad example."

The word *leadership* is something of an anathema to creative folks as it invokes an image of authority and order over the chaos that we thrive upon. Whether the image is of a person wearing an immaculate pinstriped suit or a distant figure in a large auditorium with a booming voice, leaders are generally respectfully disrespected by the creative class. For instance, an irate undergraduate student recently came up to me at an exhibition opening and said, "You know, a lot of us students and faculty don't like what you are doing with the strategic planning conversations." I asked him to continue. "You are trying to get us to work together, and we're artists. We aren't joiners and don't want to swim with the pack." I saw this as a valid point of view and asked the young man to present this viewpoint to the planning groups. "You don't get it," he replied astutely, "That would make me a joiner by definition."

Early on in my career I had the good fortune of knowing an unusual creative leader, the great Mr. Naomi Enami, who broke down many of these stereotypes for me. Mr. Enami was one of the world's first multimedia producers, predating the rise of the Web; he had a sense of showmanship that rivaled Lady Gaga's in pomp and style. But I witnessed on countless occasions how Mr. Enami could effortlessly switch his manner from Lady Gaga to Donald Trump as needed. He always had a few suits tucked away in his closet to switch into "the Donald," for when he needed a socially acceptable uniform for meticulously crafting deals with business executives.

Mr. Enami would walk into the studio at 3 am boldly announcing, "If I am here, everything is okay!" and we'd all suddenly wake up and be reenergized. A few minutes after he'd say this, he'd lie on the floor in the middle of the studio and instantly fall asleep. Mr. Enami is the one who first made me aware that there are all kinds of leaders out there—wacky, brilliant, and above all, impactful. He fell ill a few years ago, and I know that his example inspires me in the work I do today as president.

> Being prepared isn't a matter of how much you practice.
  It's about knowing that even if you fail, you won't give up.

In spite of the many recent financial challenges at my institution and in our world, my excitement in serving as president of RISD has remained extremely high. Sure, some days haven't been as pleasant as others, and I when I see veteran presidents of other institutions manage difficult situations with an elegance that only past experience can bring, I am certainly envious. But having had the experience of distinct careers as an academic, scientist, engineer, designer, and artist, I've been fortunate to know the awkwardness that comes with initially not fitting perfectly into a foreign role.

In the early 1990s, after I had completed a PhD in design studies, I was at a party in Tokyo where I heard a veteran designer tell his colleagues in Japanese (which he perhaps thought I didn't understand), "John's an engineer from MIT and he thinks he can be a designer now." I now count this person as a solid friend, and I know I've earned his respect by persevering and ultimately prospering in the field, with my designs now miraculously residing in many major museum collections. I guess I'm a believer that you can always learn when you're not willing to give up seeking out something new.

> Work is easier when its just work; it's much harder when you actually care.

There's this wonderful thing called "work" that takes an enormous amount of time in your life when you are lucky enough to have it. Sometimes the work is all work and no play. For instance, growing up working closely beside my parents before and after school in their tofu-making business every day from 3 am to 6 pm—that was the hardest work I've experienced in my life. Given the mechanical nature of the labor, I expected my father to sometimes want to take a break or cut himself some slack, but he exacted the highest quality in his work every day. He wasn't driven by making money—he could have sold the product for more, but he thought "the price is just"—so it wasn't clear to me why he worked so hard. The reason became evident when a customer came by and wanted to thank my father for making tofu with a craftsmanship that could no longer be found in Japan. Dad was always a fairly unemotional man, but I caught a glimpse of him smiling as he walked away. I asked him what "craftsmanship" was. He replied, "It's working like you care."

It is this passion for one's work that I've taken into all my endeavors: making images, books, computer chips, skateboards, jackets, circuit boards, Web sites, computer programs, lighting, tables, sculptures, paintings, and a variety of other "things" as an artist, designer, and technologist. I've just begun to take this curiosity into the space of leading an institution. It has been a journey of realizing not only the limits of creative thinking, but its possibilities as well.

In my first years as "suddenly" president of RISD, I have tried to pour as much play, passion, and creativity into the act of leading as is humanly possible. Along the way I've already learned countless lessons about communication, teamwork, and the importance of holding on to my own sense of perspective—lessons that I have tried to crystallize in the moment through the act of microblogging, or "tweeting." I've collected these microlessons here to try to see what macrolessons will be revealed through their aggregation. Please come along on this journey of micro and macro with me.

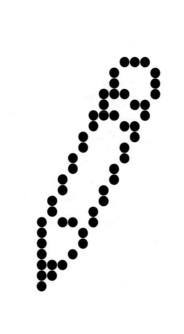

Creative as Leader

When I meet with politicians around Providence, Rhode Island, where RISD is located, I often ask them if they have any RISD interns working for them. Their reaction is often one of amusement: "No, I have interns from Brown University or Providence College, but not RISD. I don't need people drawing pictures for me." I respond with an explanation that the students I see every day at RISD work extremely hard and with unparalleled passion, and that they have a set of unique perspectives that can help any of the politicians communicate to a broader range of their constituents. And they'll often say, "Sounds great. Introduce me." It feels great to be able to open their eyes to the opportunity of seeing a creative perspective.

Coming from a creative background, I originally experienced people dismissing me in a similar way. What I've found instead—and how I feel about the students here at RISD—is that we have a different perspective on leadership coming from backgrounds in art and design. We artists and designers aren't afraid to get our hands dirty in the process of making works of art, and that same unbridled spirit can feed naturally into the challenges of leadership. A creative leader is someone who leads with dirty hands, much the way an artist's hands are often literally dirty with paint.

GETTING DIRTY

> When people ask if I've stopped designing I say, "No. I'm designing how to talk about/with/for our #RISD community."

Designers are trained to solve problems through making and iterating. When faced with a problem, they immediately pick up a pen and start to diagram, or build working models out of paper or prototype how something looks and works on the computer screen. If designers can't see it with their own eyes, then it's not real to them. Artists are no different in their fearlessness to get their hands dirty, and strive to create something new and meaningful that is driven by how they feel. As a description of a leader, however, someone who is "hands-on and emotionally driven" sounds like a recipe for a perfectly dislikable, irrational, micromanaging boss.

A few years back, I awoke from surgery to have my doctor tell me that the physiological situation inside my body wasn't what he had expected. Once he opened me up, things weren't as he anticipated, so he had to change course midstream. He said to me in a reassuring tone, "I tried something new and I hope it works!" Naturally, I wasn't too thrilled. In certain situations, you want to feel that the person in charge has it all under control. So I've been careful to approach my journey at RISD as a balance between the artist within me who looks to experiment, and the more systematic thinker who was trained at engineering and business school.

> Doing right matters more than being right.

Artists don't distinguish between the act of making something and the act of thinking about it—thinking and making evolve together in an emergent, concurrent fashion. As a result, when approaching a project, an artist often doesn't seem to plan it out She just goes ahead and begins, all the while collecting data that inform how she will continue. A large part of what drives her confidence to move forward is her faith in her ability to course correct and improvise as she goes.

For an artist, "doing the right thing" isn't about logically selecting from a set of evaluated options, but is about feeling what is right *in the moment*. For me as president, the only way to fully understand the moment, or context, is to jump in and try to understand the day-to-day workings of RISD firsthand. So I've done everything from serving food at the cafeteria, to carrying the luggage of new students arriving on campus, to making breakfast for faculty, to delivering donuts to the campus public safety officers. Some have criticized these efforts as "unpresidential," while others have welcomed seeing their leader get into the trenches.

I've learned that this leadership style isn't entirely limited to artists. One of our groundskeepers compared me to a beloved interim president at RISD who would walk everywhere around campus—boiler room, studio, kitchen—and wanted to experience everything himself. When I finally caught up with Mr. Louis Fazzano I asked, "Did you need to see everything because you are an artist?" He smiled and said, "No, I'm just a former hospital administrator who believes in managing by walking around. It's the only way to feel the whole system ... and also to be felt." Mr. Fazzano reminded me that not all traditional leaders keep their hands clean, ensconced in office fortresses tucked away from everyone else.

> @johnmaeda was asked by a student debating a choice in major
  as what she is good at doing versus what she wants to do.

Owning the perspective of an artist in the way that I lead has enabled me to understand the nature of art even better. At lunch and dinner I sometimes sit in the dining halls with students to hear what is on their minds. Sometimes I hear their concerns, but no matter the tenor of the conversation, I find myself learning something new about my institution and the agility of our young artists' minds.

One time I sat with a young woman who said to me, "I've been waiting for you to sit with me, as I have something to confess." With the initial awkwardness of the moment I immediately regretted my choice of lunch buddies, but I stayed and listened nonetheless. She went on, "You know, it is March right now of my freshman year, but I remember arriving last term—I was completely disoriented and unsure of what my professors wanted." I asked her to go on. "So now that it's my second term, I know where things are on campus, I have great friends—and I can't help but feel guilty." Now I was puzzled. "Why?" I asked. "Well," she said, "because it's easy for me now."

I discussed this later with my Provost, Jessie Shefrin, a teacher of art for more than 25 years and an especially articulate spokesperson for the mind of an artist. Jessie responded matter-of-factly, "It's because all artists yearn to struggle. Without it, they don't feel *alive*." There is tremendous elegance in this thought; to me, it explains why artists so often choose to make themselves uncomfortable instead of just doing what they may already be good at doing. The artist in me chose to leave the comfort of a tenured professorship, and I feel vulnerable and alive again.

> The upside of overworking is in those rare cases where you feel
  you actually got something done.

Another hallmark of the artist is the superhuman intensity that drives her work. It's certainly in high supply on the RISD campus. It is often pointed out that RISD really stands for "Reason I'm Sleep Deprived"—a claim that I can personally attest for given the many tired students I've observed here, face down on the floor, who have labored passionately for their final critiques or exhibitions. A few days after the opening of a retrospective of my work in Tokyo, I myself was hospitalized because of overwork. There were other similar episodes in my life that were simply stupid but also simply consistent with what artists do all the time—pursue high personal rewards with only the tiniest chance of success.

> @johnmaeda is reflecting on the difference between doing something
  just to do it, vs. doing something that leads to bigger, other somethings.

Artists are hyperaware of their surroundings, and it's often hard to focus when the noise of the world tastes so delicious. For me,

I'm attracted to the latest trends, buzzwords, and technology tools like shiny objects—I find it impossible to turn away. Similarly, when talking to parents of RISD students I hear stories about their children's ability to stare at the beautiful reflections of the sun hitting the ice in a water glass during dinner, or to draw from memory a beautiful garden they overlooked on a summer trip from many years prior. Rather than being driven to distraction by our senses, the challenge of the artist is to channel this sensitivity into a broader context.

Perhaps the best advice I received as a young professor at MIT was when I mentioned to my mentor Professor Whitman Richards, a giant in the field of cognitive science, that I wanted to address some issues of faculty politics at MIT head on. Professor Richards gently responded, "John, don't think about MIT. Think about the world. Broaden your focus as far as possible."

> Leading by doing ceases to be leading when you are doing more than leading.

The primary challenge for a leader who is a natural doer is to discover the balance between the two; otherwise the specter of micromanagement can easily make a guest appearance. This is the downside of being a "dirty-hands leader." Getting too down and dirty means that you're taking away the work that's to be done by the people that you lead. Some folks will be happy that they can go on a coffee break while their boss does their work, but others will feel undermined and robbed.

I've learned I need to find some dirt of my own to play in. Becky astutely pointed out to me one day that the work of understanding and leading RISD that I engage in on a day-to-day basis *is* my dirty work—so I've come to learn and appreciate the beauty of getting "metadirty." Granted, it's a different kind of dirt: One time some RISD students whispered to me that I can't be considered trustworthy because "you look too clean in those perfectly white shirts you wear. It's not normal."

PRETTY IN PICTURES

> Recalls being told long ago that "a picture is worth a thousand words ...
> and yet it takes words to say that."

X	Y	X	Y	X	Y
47.0	11.0	90.3	89.8	90.3	49.5
50.7	24.4	65.7	69.6	85.0	64.0
53.5	39.3	59.6	62.1	75.3	78.7
85.3	55.3	40.0	41.1	62.4	86.4
43.9	68.4	16.7	13.8	46.9	90.1
76.6	82.5	9.8	8.49	31.8	86.5
31.5	88.0	25.5	24.8	17.1	72.2
87.0	12.1	87.1	85.1	12.0	57.0
30.0	31.0	58.1	55.9	9.48	42.3
30.6	68.5	47.7	52.5	19.5	24.7
69.0	39.6	81.5	79.0	30.5	16.0
9.0	51.8	22.0	22.4	46.4	12.0
15.9	12.1	72.0	73.0	63.3	13.7
95.5	24.9	46.8	44.2	78.4	20.1
11.9	89.3	32.3	34.6	86.7	33.6

Edward Tufte's hugely popular books on visualizing information give testament to the power of images to create understanding from chaos. Tufte is well known for highlighting how data displayed with misleading images led to the space shuttle disaster of 1986. The ability to make sense with a simple picture is powerful. Consider the above example of 90 pieces of information that all seem to fit no particular pattern.

When they are revealed in visual form, clear relationships can be ascertained; the first set is randomly dispersed, the second set is a line, and the third is a circle.

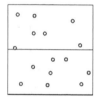

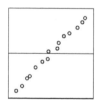

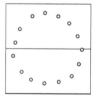

These kind of pictures demonstrate the power of visual representations when used to effectively illuminate a data set. In recent years, projects like the open-source visualization project Processing, founded by Ben Fry and Casey Reas, have enabled artists and designers to participate in visualizing complex data on an even grander scale. This category of work shows that images may not work perfectly to reveal specific information, but they can often provide a bird's-eye view that would not be possible otherwise. Whether it's Fry's own work visualizing the entire human genome or Burak Arikan's visualization of financial transactions, seeing the whole picture for the first time can change how you feel and move you to action.

Drawing inspiration from this field, I spent the first six months or so of my presidency trying to interpret RISD's organization and systems visually. It was only after I'd produced hundreds of diagrams that my intuition finally kicked in, and I was able to start to see the big picture of how the organization worked.

Ultimately, though, I realized that the value of these pictures was limited and, although they might be able to win a design award, and helped me personally, they more often lost my audience's attention. The complex business of propelling an organization forward rarely lends itself to the same treatment as a column of numbers. Any work involving people, and the relationships between them, just doesn't work that way.

> Problem with drawing a simple explanatory picture is by the time
  it makes sense, it's too complex to reuse.

Like many visually minded people, I seek to draw explanatory images to find ways to communicate a complex concept more effectively. During any given meeting, my natural inclination is to find a marker and a blank surface upon which to diagram what is being said. The problem is that not everyone is a visually oriented learner—even, I've found, at an art school.

Every time I try to diagram some organizational phenomena or strategy, the resulting pretty picture generally fails to create any lasting understanding. Much like movies, diagrams are more meaningful when you are there to witness the "making-of" experience or any other "live" means of presentation. We love to be there at the very moment of conception of an idea, and when we're not, we're less likely to be excited by the idea (because it doesn't feel like our own). There is something to be said for sitting right there and watching the drawing unfold—it can make the spoken narrative clearer.

At the very end of an intense diagramming session that has revealed every possible magnificent detail, there is always the moment of excitement and reckoning that warrants, "Wait, wait … let me take a photo of this with my mobile phone." But when you show it to someone else a week or two later, it no longer makes any sense. Watching something being made is a powerful way to understand a concept; trying to decode just the final result, no matter how simple and visually elegant, demands an explanation of how it came to be.

> Children's drawings reveal visual truths we've let reality
  fool ourselves into denying.

Many nonvisual people suffer from the opposite problem—rather than overdrawing, they feel they don't know what to draw or how best to draw it. The best counteracting force in nature for this disposition is to look at pictures drawn by children. Kids excel at drawing from their mental model of the world, which can either make complete sense or be absolutely absurd. Whether depicting a horse with five eyes and twelve legs or a dog with the tail of a squirrel, kids' drawings immediately transport you to a world where anything can exist if you let it. Provost Shefrin likes to say, "When things are turned upside down you get the chance to truly see something for what it is." So I often see her turn her head sideways to stop making sense of something in front of her, in pursuit of finding something else that she may have missed.

CRITIQUE ME, PLEASE!

> Competency results in success results in complacency results in failure results in learning how to be competent again.

At MIT I once overheard my colleagues commend a professor not for his superb command of knowledge, but for his humbling ability to plainly express his own lack of understanding. "Instead of bullsh*tting," they said, "he's unafraid to answer a question with, 'I don't know.'" In my opinion, what was so astonishing is not that the professor would do this, but that acknowledging one's weakness was seen as so unusual. Most professors rely upon their position to assert "absolute truths" backed by their own standing in their field. But this professor never used his superior position as an advantage, and instead he was able to constantly learn and grow from his own vulnerability.

> When I can convert a "meeting" into a "critique," although it opens me
  to all criticisms, I oddly feel more at ease.

Taking a page from former NYC mayor Ed Koch, I open some of my meetings with a simple question, "How am I doing?" People often wonder if I'm being facetious, but I'm truly looking for the opportunity to be critiqued—an uncomfortable but effective practice for any respectable artist or designer. For an artist, a critique is the opportunity to see if others connect with the questions that underlie his work, to see if the work's original intentions and integrity shine through. For designers, it is an opportunity to improve the efficacy of their work by testing whether it is intuitive to others.

A good critique reveals your blind spots, but it can also be difficult to recover from, so approaching honest feedback with an open mind is everything. I once was at a faculty gathering where I was asked for my opinion about learning. I forget exactly what I said, but I received a sharp drub in response, something like, "You really need to distinguish between learning and knowledge." It didn't make sense to me at first, but hours later I began to appreciate the implications of this critical lesson.

I've learned that the higher up you go in an organization, the less likely people are to say what's on their mind, for fear of retribution. However, without provocation it's impossible to learn new things, and thus I find that direct critique is the fastest way to learn how to improve. Provost Shefrin says, "Critique teaches you to listen hard to others' criticism so you can listen hardest to yourself." So, being cognitively jostled, or "brain-dissed," can sometimes be good for you.

> Feedback makes the mind grow stronger.

Part of the challenge inherent in welcoming feedback is dealing with the inevitable expectation that you will act on all of the input given to you. Since opinions vary greatly, this is practically impossible: If you choose the path suggested by person A, it may directly counteract a suggestion by person B. In the event that person A and person B give you two distinct ideas that you don't necessarily like, and meanwhile you discover option C, then you've done even worse by A and B since you didn't heed either of them. Yet it is often input from A and B that got you to C, so they were a necessary part of the journey.

Sometimes a voice from left field can set you right—so I have open office hours and breakfasts where faculty, staff, and students can come and visit me individually. I find that being exposed to many opinions opens the doors of possibility. In the end, it's about learning to hear your own voice as a leader. Many artists make art of a personal nature; it is how they learn to see themselves on their own terms, not by just what they see in the mirror. The more kinds of mirrors artists can use to see their work, the sharper the image reflecting back at them becomes.

For example, I once had a solo exhibition at the London Institute of Contemporary Arts. After the show opened, the director came to me with great joy to share a special review of my work. My immediate thought was that it might be from an important European art critic, but the director clarified that it was from a custodian on the night shift. Seeing my initial look of disappointment, he asked me how often I had gotten a constructive comment from the noncuratorial staff at a museum. I told him,

"Never." He told me to rejoice and to consider myself lucky. And sure enough, after hearing the custodian's comments, a whole new world opened up for me. She gave me a chance to see a very special mirror of my work that I may have otherwise ignored owing to my limited view.

> I'd rather be green and growing instead of ripe, ready to rot.

Artists are natural conduits of change, transforming raw materials into finished expressions: from a blank canvas into a still-life flower, or from mathematical algorithms into computer art. They constantly seek to find new and improved means to transform ideas into reality. Learning something new means finding not just a new way to see the world, but often a new way to change the world—which for the artist is the modus operandi.

Ever since I've become president, people often approach me with a pained look on their face and ask earnestly, "How are you doing?" My answer is generally a simple but honest, "I'm learning." Then comes the inevitable moment of confusion, as they were expecting the usual upbeat perspective of a CEO. They say something like, "Oh, it's that bad?" The exchange forces me to clarify how excited I am to be a leader right now because I love to learn. There is nothing I'd rather be doing than learning. It often isn't an easy task and I've made mistakes. But the artist in me accepts the possibility of being wrong for the opportunity it provides to learn. I believe *anything* you do will be more wrong until you learn how to do it more right. So, I'm learning and growing.

INTUITION COUNTS

> We live in an age where data matter increasingly more than intuition.
  But that's just my intuition talking ...

Although data can make a compelling case for something, data
rarely create the emotions needed to spur people into action.
Statistics about global warming were always compelling, but
it wasn't until Al Gore's movie about our environment, *An In-
convenient Truth,* gave a narrative context to the data that the
movement catapulted into the mainstream. The importance
of narrative was reinforced at a dinner I attended at the 2010
Davos World Economic Forum. There I sat next to a woman,
Zainab Salbi, who contributed a particularly memorable comment: "Stories trump statistics." In other words, it's more
important to convey the reason *why* you are presenting the
numbers instead of the intricacies of the numbers themselves.
Telling a good story isn't a quantitative skill, but it is a skill that
requires intuition about what your audience wants to hear and
how to tell it in a compelling manner. Artists are uniquely gifted
with storytelling abilities using text, images, dance, music, or
other forms of expression. The emotional richness of these experiences, driven by an artist's intuition about what to express,
makes for a particularly compelling case.

> Art is about the unexpecte

Artists rely on their intuition much more than those who are
analytically trained. Analytical people tend to take a complex

problem and reduce it to its component parts in an effort to solve it step by step. Artists, however, attempt to make giant leaps to a solution, seeming to ignore all constraints. By making those leaps, they sometimes miss the solution completely. But they are not afraid to miss the target.

At first rational glance, it is easy to discount this approach as being simply impractical. I know that in my own transition from engineering school to art school in Japan, I didn't understand why my new colleagues would simply jump to a conclusion without defining the foundation for their leap. So it often bothered me when they would get it right more often than I. Duchamp's infamous *Fountain*—a plain porcelain urinal— seemed ridiculous at first, but its brilliance came from the time and place in which it was presented. Duchamp's controversial leap to reject figurative norms represented a certain timeliness that artists seem to feel in their bones. So the artist's intuition is different than merely being random—it's as simple as paying attention to the moment and being true to what he truly believes.

I know this feeling quite well from my own work in making art for the desktop computer. When I created a computer program that rendered a black square that would morph and move as you talk to it, many people thought I should be using the predominant tool of the time, Adobe Photoshop, instead. I even had a design professor in Japan call me into his office so that he could yell at me for an hour to say that my work would never amount to anything. So, I still find it hard to believe when I walk into the Museum of Modern Art and see a computer with my black square jiggling about in response to people's voices hanging there on the wall. I'm glad I followed my intuition down the many unexpected paths that have presented themselves to me.

So much change has happened in our world in the last few decades because of information technology. When people ask me how to cope with these changes, I suggest that they look to artists for inspiration in how they actively apply their intuition. Solicit critique and actively sketch out the big picture so that your feelings can work in tandem with the surrounding context. In the end, intuition helps you manage the unexpected, because you've been unafraid to *feel* the possibilities. Be confident that a leap can be taken, and that you will land standing. Artists do it all the time. We aren't afraid to fail, but we certainly are afraid to end up as people who don't want to get their hands dirty in the act of trying.

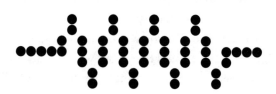

3

Technologist as Leader

A leader's job is to get people on board with his vision—and he'll try whatever tools are at his disposal to do it. I've gone about this leadership challenge in a variety of ways, but I must admit that my strongest influence is my training in information technology from MIT.

Computers make it so simple to communicate. It's just as easy to send a hundred messages to a hundred people in different countries as it is to send an e-mail to a single person in the next city. Social media like blogs, Facebook, and Twitter have made it even easier to broadcast to thousands. Ironically, though, with all the communication technologies at our disposal today, it's still difficult to get a message across to the person sitting right next to you in a reliable fashion.

While I was interviewing at RISD, students told me that they were tired of getting e-mails from "the administration" that spoke about the importance of community, but which at the very bottom read, "Please do not reply to this e-mail message." "Surely I can do better than that," I thought to myself. I believed that it was possible to leverage communication methods I knew well—like e-mail and blogging—in the service of administering an institution.

I've come to realize, however, that while technology may make it more convenient to communicate, it doesn't improve our ability to get a point across. Sure, it's great to profess your love remotely via Skype or to let the world know about a new app via a blog. But when it comes to communicating to a large organization, an e-mail blast or a blog post doesn't always cut it. Technology answers only part of the problem—the part that refers to the technical question of delivering a message—and there usually are bigger problems to deal with. First, there's content: *What* you say, and whether you're expressing it clearly, is more important than how you choose to say it. Second, there's context: *Why* you're saying it, and what e-mail boasts in convenience is counteracted by the sensory deprivation of plain text. So the content has to be especially fine-tuned in order to make up for the missing emotional context. I find that it very rarely is.

LET ME BE CLEAR

> @johnmaeda is happy to have learned from Provost Shefrin the important
  distinction between being transparent ... and being clear.

The open-source software movement has a certain beauty to it; the promise is that by exposing all the code, not only can anyone reproduce the behavior of a software program, but anyone can improve the behavior of a program. Also, making the computer code readable by everyone allows for collective policing of un-ethical behavior (e.g., inserting code that could transmit one's credit card information unbeknownst to the user). In the last few years we've seen the Obama administration enact similar "open-source" approaches to government. Federal appropriation requests are now openly visible on the Web and the White House now posts online records of all its visitors for the public to see. The culture we live in has forced the idea of transparency to live front and center in today's definition of ethical behavior.

The assumption behind increased transparency is that having access to all of the facts will make everyone rest easier. But as I've learned in countless ways over the past few years, mere exposure to information doesn't equate with true understanding. I can certainly read lines of Linux code as a trained engineer, but I have no idea how to modify it without breaking it. To get to an understanding of how it all works would take me a long, long time. In other words, transparency is great, but it doesn't necessarily provide clarity.

> "For example" is an exemplary tool for achieving clarity.

A few months ago, I addressed a large group of RISD parents about this issue of transparency versus clarity. A father stood up in the front row and introduced himself as an English professor, and he shared a simple tool he teaches his students about achieving clarity. He said the simple trick is to use "for example." Facts are usually much more useful when presented with examples that enable an audience to connect with information at a deeper level. A "for example" is often what we need to make the light bulb of clarity go on not just for your audience, but for you as the leader.

> "Clarity dissolves resistance."-Heath Bros. http://j.mp/bLdaA6

Because I'm so accustomed to working in technology-rich environments, where people are more comfortable with e-mail than with a telephone call, I've always found a certain allure in writing the perfect e-mail. Sometimes an e-mail can feel as though it gets better and better as you write it, and by the time you're done, it comprehensively explains all the facts (i.e., it achieves transparency) but it is impossible to understand (i.e., it doesn't achieve clarity). I find you can generally predict the efficacy of your e-mail communication by the length of the message. Longer is generally bad; shorter is generally good. Usually the lightness of fewer words enables the message to travel further distances; the recipient is better able to share the content with his or her colleagues.

I also find that greater clarity is achieved by specifying the recipient of the message. E-mail can get confusing when there is a long line of people in the "To:" or "CC:" field. As an example of a different approach, in a student project on social media that I once supervised, the messaging system was programmed so that it was impossible to send a message to multiple users. Taking a page from this project, my own e-mail preference is to send an e-mail to only a single person and not to a whole bunch of people, because when you focus on a single person as the "To:" and refrain from any "CC:," she knows that she is the only one in the world that matters. It may not be the most efficient way to disseminate information, as Becky has pointed out to me, but what it lacks in efficiency I find is well made up for in improved clarity.

A LITTLE SUBTLETY GOES A LONG WAY

> The shortest communication path between two people is a straight talk.

Once I sent an e-mail to campus and received a reply from a student with the subject line, "How to really communicate with us students, idiot." I wrote back to him and we engaged in an e-mail dialogue, and it became clear that although neither my e-mail nor his was particularly effective at communicating, the fact that we were "talking" together made a world of difference.

Traditional broadcast means of communicating, such as a town hall meeting or a campus-wide e-mail, are sometimes necessary, but what I've become more and more enamored of is the simplicity of a conversation between two people. It is high-bandwidth, engaging, interactive, and, putting my fiscal hat on for a moment, *expensive*. Yet I've discovered it's the greatest tool that a leader really has and is her best chance to get a point across. As said by a colleague at a conference recently, "Less presentation, more discussion." People want to talk, and it's difficult to do so in a large offline or even online format. Even as a professor, I often wandered around the classroom or among the seats in the lecture hall to get closer to students and engage them in a dialogue.

Nowadays I try to minimize blogging and e-mail, which I had so favored when I arrived here at RISD. Because I can't see everyone personally, I often ask my direct reports to communicate information through the organization. Even though it seems so much more complicated and less efficient than an e-mail, and although the message may change as it gets passed along, it's usually delivered with the right context and in a personable manner. In the end, complex information delivered by a person usually feels better.

> The warmth of a bona fide campfire chat isn't possible online,
  but the laughter (LOL) is certainly real.

I recall being interviewed by John Hockenberry in Second Life during its heyday. My avatar clumsily "walked" down some stairs and I "sat" in an auditorium with about a hundred other avatars. Although I felt connected to some degree because I saw "myself" in a crowd of other virtual people, there was something missing. Every detail was carefully rendered—from the individual strands of hair that moisten near water, to the visual evidence of wind or even air conditioning—but for all their ability to mesmerize, virtual worlds fail to transmit the bodily warmth of a hug, the nuance of real laughter, and the incomparable commitment formed by being in the same place at the same time.

Emoticons are an interesting attempted antidote to the roboticness of the e-mails that we send out. It's hard to imagine the leader of a major corporation sending out an e-mail with a smiley in it, but without its equivalent, it's hard to read the emotion behind an electronic message. Around the time when emoticons were first "discovered" in the 1980s—don't forget it took someone to first tilt his head 90 degrees sideways to see a smiling face in :-) or 8^)—my advisor at MIT took to the alternative of a parenthetical facial expression by appropriately inserting the word "(smile)." It captures the intent without the cuteness that comes with the smiley. Not a bad idea, don't you think? (smile)

> Real communication is made by finding the specific part in you
  that *needs* to join with those same parts in others.

During the world financial crisis of 2008–2009 I gave many presentations on campus, designing slides with my own hands in painstaking detail until I felt they conveyed the point perfectly. What I realized later was that the audience wasn't necessarily paying attention to my graphics, but instead they were responding directly to the pitch of my voice. Andrew Blau, futurist and copresident of Global Business Network, once shared with me how when he enters a room as a speaker, he automatically assumes that the audience is non-English speaking, even if he is in the United States. It reminds him of the importance of his tone, hand gestures, and emphasis in his voice to give him an increased chance for success in communicating. This reinforces to me that what you say in words, numbers, or pictures matters less than how you come across as a human being.

Emotion is a real wild card in the delivery of a message—an excessive display of emotion can go the wrong way, or be just the thing that is timely and needed. A mistimed joke to an audience that isn't looking for a laugh can fall flat. Conversely, I once gave a short talk at our annual scholarship lunch where I recounted the story of one of our financial aid recipients whose mother started crying when he received his acceptance letter to RISD. He asked his mother why she was so sad, and she responded, "Because we can't afford to send you there." I felt I had slipped terribly as I started to choke up while I told the story. Slightly embarrassed, I later apologized to several members of the audience; one smiled and whispered to me, "I'm increasing my scholarship contribution. Keep up the good work."

It's not surprising to me how many of our leaders today appear expressionless and robotic—it is a means of protection from being misperceived or misunderstood. No matter what the message, however, the one thing I've learned it's most important to convey is respect—it's the prerequisite for any other kind of communication. Finding, knowing, and owning the respect that each audience deserves is the place where real communication is born.

> Sophistication is the craft of subtlety that goes noticed.

Much of how designers work and think is hidden in the details—they make infinite subtle decisions that endow a message with the ability to capture an audience's imagination. For instance, there are many choices in how a letter is written that make it a "designed object": the texture of the paper, the kind of ink, the chosen stamp, and of course the sender's handwriting. I attended a memorial service for the late Professor Richard Merkin, where I saw letters that were created as if they were the most important thing imaginable. From vintage stamps and stickers to his quirky handwritten script, it made me think about how difficult, by comparison, achieving that kind of subtlety and depth of meaning in electronic communication can be.

There are attempts to bring some of that kind of craft to electronic messages today, such as customized salutations, reply-to bars, or inline images. Yet as anyone who has received an overly perky e-mail in Comic Sans knows, these attempts quickly veer into the gaudy and overly complex. One of my most impactful e-mails to the campus was a handwritten letter that I photographed and sent as an image. Of course that doesn't meet requirements for the visually impaired, but I could see from the response that people are looking for the human touch. They're looking for the subtlety of dirt and irregularity of the hand to feel the human spirit. Subtlety is a kind of dust in the room of life that shouldn't be confused with just dirt.

I've observed an acute mastery of the subtlety of communication in the workings of my provost. To prepare for the launch of our strategic planning process, we met several times to discuss how it should feel and what it should accomplish. On the day of the launch meeting, we were about to get started when she made an odd request: "John, can you get me a few oranges?" Never one to turn down a unique request like that, I fetched an orange for her. She opened the meeting by throwing it to a participant while asking the question, "Tell us all why you are here in one sentence." After he obliged, she asked the participant to toss the orange back to her. She caught it, then threw it to another person asking the same question.

The orange went back and forth around the room and I witnessed not only Jessie's incredible pitching arm, but also what started to happen among the people in the room: They were all connecting with each other. By the time the orange had made it to everyone in that room, the meeting was well on its way to being productive. I mentioned this story to an expert in organizational development, who posited that the smell of the orange may have helped establish the cohesiveness of the group as well.

OLD-FASHIONED STILL TASTES GOOD

> Being heard lessens being hurt.

There are many ways to register your feelings online—such as a post on a blog, or an anonymous vote in an e-poll. Making a survey online takes no more than a few minutes and is an efficient way to gather a sense of people's positions on an issue. Or so I once thought when I was a young professor. The first few times I used them to cull students' opinions, the polls fell on dead ears and dead mouse-clicks. Was everyone too busy to participate? Fast-forward fifteen years and I still find an online poll to be tempting, but I know that it doesn't really do the community justice as a means to be heard.

Votes are blind, scalable, and measurable, but they are also unfortunately simplistic in their ability to capture the complexity of opinion beyond a raised or lowered hand. I was humbled by the efforts of a senior at RISD who during my first few weeks noticed my failed efforts to communicate electronically with students and organized an in-person conversation at 9 pm to see how many students might come. Roughly forty or so came. You could tell that they wanted to hear each other and to have me hear those conversations. They came from different departments and class years, and those differences were evident in how they shared their feelings in tone and demeanor. This was one of many occasions when I realized the subtleties that can be truly communicated only by using our eyes with sight, our nose with smell, and our sense of touch with a firm handshake.

SOCIAL MEDIA BREAKS BARRIERS, KIND OF

> @johnmaeda is thinking how in a world where everyone is an author, author(ity) means less.

When I first started to use Twitter, I was intrigued by the idea of a level playing field for people to give their two cents' worth. Celebrities, shopkeepers, soccer moms, CEOs, drama club geeks, and college presidents have an equal voice in the social mediaverse. At the Media Lab we lived at the forefront of technological possibilities, but we always fantasized about the moment when everyone started to use these new technologies—that was when the world would really change. During the 2008 election, there was a YouTube video with a young man in a public park registering voters. At the very end of the piece, he deadpans the camera and says, "If you are under 18, you can't vote. <insert dramatic pause> But now you can be heard." The point was that by using the Internet, young people can create a sufficient amount of noise and make a real impact without having the credentials of being legal voters.

Even though we can all now be heard, most organizations are based on a traditional hierarchy that governs communication, coordinates action, and achieves scalability and order. We aren't ready to replace the government or administrative structures with a Twitter network, nor are we ready to close down college administrations and run an entire school on Facebook. But the fact remains that we live in an age where there is a high degree of individual agency that can be aggregated on demand and disrupt the traditional notion of authority in positive ways. For example, at my first student orientation meeting, I met the organizers of the Class of 2012 Facebook group, who, rather than waiting to show up on campus to see who was in their hall, started a Google spreadsheet that was populated by each of the incoming students to make a crowdsourced map of the housing assignments. Such examples abound, and they will challenge the existence and efficacy of existing administrative structures.

> Flat is the new black

When I was announced as president in 2008, I immediately began to receive a stream of e-mails from people who wanted to have a private conversation or coffee with me. This was all happening during the last election, and President Obama's message of transparency created a mood towards more open conversations rather than closed-room ones. So rather than setting up coffee dates, we launched a blog where I could talk with the entire community in the open—to exclude no one and get to know everyone. An MIT alumni colleague at Harvard Business School and expert on corporate blogging, Andrew McAfee, recommended that one day a week the blog should be anonymous, and so "Anonymous Tuesdays" was inaugurated. Every Tuesday, any employee can choose to comment on any post anonymously, without revealing his or her identity to the community or the administration.

Two years later I don't regret starting this blog, but I've definitely curtailed my own participation on it. I've learned that by replying personally, I was undermining people in my own chain of command. In other words, managers in the hierarchy serve specific roles in communicating with the campus and I now believe that the president really has no business responding on their behalf. Being aware of the many conversations happening on campus *is* the business of the president, so I spend a great deal of time listening and learning from conversations that happen both online and offline to understand my community.

> Until you can serve pizza or drinks over the Web, a social media portal
  to foster true collaboration will be so-so.

There are many, myself included, whose first inclination is to believe that everything can be fixed with some kind of Web site. Have a communication problem? Post the information online. But once the site is built, there's the awkward realization that it's not meaningful unless people visit it. Nor does it truly come alive unless someone is constantly populating the Web site with refreshed content.

I had thought that Facebook had solved all of this because it is constantly living and breathing, kind of like a 24/7 café of many minds. At the time I started at RISD, I think I was one of a tiny number of presidents with a personal Facebook page— I saw it as a great opportunity to connect with students. But after a while I realized that it was more useful in connecting with alumni from afar than with the students on my campus.

"Why?" I wondered. After all, I'd watched my own high-school daughters constantly glued to their Facebook pages. The students' unanimous response was, "I'm not on Facebook as much because all my friends are *here* now." In high school Facebook provides an escape back to their school friends while at home, whereas on a residential campus like RISD's, students are living together with their friends and are in constant contact anyway.

So I've given up on Facebook as the best means to pull people together and have turned to a more traditional technology: free food. Since my years as a professor, I have seen the two words "free pizza" scribbled onto a sign or in the subject line of an e-mail as a powerful motivator to convene large numbers of students who might not be inspired by other possible two-word combinations like "global warming" or "nuclear disarmament." As a friend told me once, food and fire have brought people together since the beginning of time. I'm not so good at making a fire, but luckily I can cook, and I've used that skill on a variety of occasions. Making people work together can be fairly challenging, but getting them to eat together is somehow vastly easier. A meal is often a catalyst for a conversation that can lead to a collaboration, and a meal is a natural happening to signify closure when the collaboration has completed. And yes, I've gained weight since beginning as president so I can literally feel the collaboration happening.

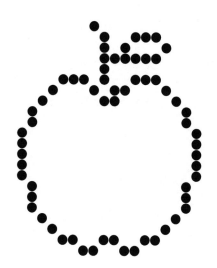

4

Professor as Leader

One of the many privileges of being a professor, and also a subtle social developmental handicap, is that you get to be your own self. Academic advancement is largely a question of whether you have individually made a significant contribution to your field. As a result, because I was never big on team sports and for most of my life have worked as a professional "lone wolf," I'm embarrassed to say that I had never felt what it's like to be on a team.

Around 2004, my interest was piqued when I learned that the men's U.S. Olympics basketball team, which boasted many of the world's greatest players, didn't win the gold medal. I found this absolutely perplexing. It awoke me to the fact that there could be a difference between a group of great individuals and a team that could win. I came to RISD because I wanted to be on a winning team: I had the audacity to believe I could figure out how to lead one myself.

STARTING A TEAM

> Standing in the same room is a big, big start.

A formative experience for me came in 2001, when I took on a leadership position at MIT for which I was completely unprepared. I quickly learned a lot about what I didn't know and subsequently stepped down from the position to seek the training that I lacked. I wasn't ready. A key lesson I learned from that experience was how being the leader in name doesn't mean that people will listen to you or want to be on your team. So I picked up a variety of minor leadership roles on campus—such as running committees and events—to find out how to create the conditions to form a team that people *wanted* to be on.

I've learned that the first step in forming any team is to resolve the most basic challenge: getting folks to take the big step away from just being themselves (the thing we all know best) and joining something larger (the thing we fear may let us down). Much is written about how to motivate people through that awkward transition from "me" to "we" using carrots (rewarding with incentives) or sticks (punishing misbehavior). But before either can be employed, the smell of the carrot needs to be in range or the stick within reach. Said differently, becoming a team starts with an individual making a choice to volunteer themselves for a collective cause.

In my own experience as a professor, the first question that came to my mind when asked to join a team was always, "Who else is on it?" In academia, where turnover is low and most of the available teammates are more than familiar, I found that ancient memories of some skirmish from decades prior led many faculty to a natural disinclination to joiner-ship. It wasn't until I was thrust into a leadership role and experienced firsthand the challenges of trying to lead that I began my commitment to becoming a better follower.

Alhough this may sound simplistic, I'm certain that the best way to start is just to get everyone you want on the team into the same room. Whether brought by duty or desire, once people are in the same room, they've assumed the basic stance of being a team—which is to be together. Preconceived negative opinions don't evaporate, but at least negativity can mix with positivity in the room, which by electrical principles results in the neutralizing of the respective +/– charges. I now consider this the most basic concept to leading a team.

> Community and Communication are advanced by simply recognizing what lies in Common (c,o,mm, n).

Once everyone is in the same room, the next challenge of getting a team to function is getting its members to talk to each other. Ironically, the only reason many of them have shown up is that someone in a position of authority is scheduled to be there, but her presence usually makes everyone uncomfortable. The longer I've been president, and the more aware of my role I've become, the more I realize how I can change the course of a conversation artificially by what I do or say. So I see myself becoming a predictably restrained, stiff leader—which is unlikely to improve a situation where you want people to be comfortable and to talk with each other. So what's a leader to do?

Shortly after Dr. Frank Moss arrived at the Media Lab to assume his new role as director, a junior faculty member tragically and suddenly died. In his second week, Frank addressed the memorial service. Although we didn't all know him very well, I saw him capable of a honed CEO-ability to connect with his people with extraordinary elegance and humanity in a time of great emotional crisis. What was important was that he revealed that a leader has all of the same feelings as everyone else—he saddens when he feels the hurt in others, chooses to always be gracious, and finds what is tastefully funny. So as much as I know I need to be careful in what I say, I still believe that the only way a leader has a chance to connect is to start by revealing her own humanity.

That said, sitting at the head of the table, the leader also needs to exude and translate the confidence necessary for the group to build positive momentum. I find it's all about striking the right balance. If you look like you're botoxed and emotionless, or have been hit by a poisonous dart by Batman's archnemesis, the Joker—always smiling—then you aren't striking the right balance. I find myself discretely pinching myself at those tables to remind myself that I'm just a person with feelings like everyone else, and that it's okay to be human.

> @johnmaeda is thinking how when your arms are crossed, ideas are deflected from entering your heart. So, open your arms.

I once worked with a fellow who had the habit of sitting in a meeting with his arms perpetually crossed. I was often asked why that person was inherently against everything that was discussed at the meeting, which, based upon private conversations I had with him, I knew not be true at all. People commented on his body language, but it turned out he had a medical condition that was alleviated by crossing his arms, and he wasn't aware of the psychological impression of the gesture. I could easily understand this because I had a similar experience. I recall being in a meeting roughly ten years ago where I made a fist-like gesture as a means to alleviate the pain I regularly experience from carpal-tunnel syndrome. I understand that some people commented that I was unusually tense at the meeting, what with my fist held so tightly. Since then I have tried to be more careful with my gestures. Open hands lead to the open arms necessary to bring people together.

> The difference between a community and an audience is where
  you choose to stand on the stage.

A sense of community is formed by active, impromptu conversations that speak the truth—conversations where everyone has an opportunity to talk and be heard. This is easier said than done: The question is how to achieve one of these conversations. To some extent, it depends on the level of mutual respect (or disrespect!) among the group. The rest has to do with all of the subtle distinctions of how roles play out in the room. Who is joining a conversation, and who is just listening in? Who has a speaking part, and who has been relegated to the part of a rock or tree that sits silently? Who is contributing, and who is merely interfering? It's important that those on stage, or around a table, know their part, otherwise they can end up unintentionally obstructing each other. A community that learns to work as a team can start winning games instead of just watching them—so every conversation can be an exercise in how to get there.

> "... create a type of org that is capable of continuously dissolving conflict while increasing choice."—Russell Ackoff

When I was a young professor, I often felt that professors treated arguing like a full-contact sport. Outsiders would initially take offense, until they realized that this is what we do in academia—we debate and question until no stone has gone unturned, and at the end we see if there is a valid new discovery to be made. Sometimes nothing at all is discovered, which is also okay, so long as there has been integrity in the process of the debate. I recall sitting with a physics professor who began a conversation with me by asking quite bluntly, "So, why do all your designs suck?" Despite its appearances, I understood that his comment wasn't an insult, but was his simple way of starting a constructive debate on design.

Groups within an organization can also start productive conflict that serves to bring a group of people to a new level. For instance, when I was at the Media Lab, the former head of a major industrial research lab told me how jealous she was of academic labs like ours where each research group had its own unique identity. In the lab she ran, there could be no such differentiation between groups because the whole point was to emphasize that everyone was on the same team. Without the ability to create some degree of individualism, she felt there was less of a possibility for creativity to flourish. In academia, we are accustomed to proud individualism and fierce internal competition as a source of our creativity, as well as a source of productive conflict. However, it is also the underlying obstacle to building a broader, all-encompassing team for the institution.

HUDDLING IS WORK

> In the best meetings there are usually more wannacomes than havetacomes.

If you haven't guessed already, I am a person who doesn't naturally care for meetings. I have always been more of a deadlines person—I've always lived to hunker down on the doing. When I switched to an administrative role, however, I could see that I quickly had to become a meetings person. As I became inculcated in the process of running large meetings, the difference between people who wanted-to-be-there and people who had-to-be-there was always striking. (And don't forget the people who are just there for the free food—they're in their own *"wannaeat"* category.) The *wannacomes* are identifiable by the way they sit in their chairs, leaning forward to participate, whereas the *havetacomes* are checking their e-mail as if you won't notice.

As someone who was rarely in the *wannacome* category myself, I think that increasing the *wannacomes* to *havetacomes* ratio is a matter of increasing the effectiveness of the meeting while decreasing its length. It's better to leave people wanting more. For example, when I first inherited the leadership of a longstanding council at MIT, I was surprised by how the majority of its meeting time was spent with members commiserating about their various negative experiences linked to the topic of the council. No work could get done because there was so much personal discussion. After a few months, I removed the unofficial commiseration component of the meeting, and attendance at this meeting quickly improved. Keeping the meeting focused on getting real work done is usually welcome, but it is often difficult to engineer when the work to be done is not made clear for everyone. You know you are on the right path in running your meeting when, at the conclusion, people start saying with sincere regret, "I wish this meeting was a little longer"—which is preferable to the opposite reaction of, "This meeting is way too long."

In an effort to reflect my leadership style (and meet more efficiently), I've recently removed my office's personal executive washroom and have replaced it with a waist-height meeting table with no chairs. I'm curious about how holding so-called "stand-up meetings" to increase efficiency and informality—a method popularized by Google and other software companies—will translate to my environment. In addition, I've taken a page from Mayor Bloomberg's playbook of a "bullpen-style" office so that I sit with my staff in the same office space as a way to build teamwork and collaboration. Whether these redesigns will be successful or not I am frankly unsure, but I will be certain to report on it at a later date.

> When the right people are all in the right room with the right timing they can make the right decision ... right now.

When the work is simple, and an organization has well-established rules and processes, people don't have to meet as much because the answers can be found "in the book" and aren't the subject of general debate. That is, meetings exist to promote discussion; rules exist to demote discussion. The best rules and processes remove the need to reinvent the wheel while retaining the ability to add human judgment. Such rules and processes can acknowledge that it is a good idea to meet from time to time to examine how a rule or process may or may not apply. There's a necessary balance—when an organization has to revisit everything in the rule book at every turn, then it comes to a standstill.

I caught a great quote on Twitter last year by Kim Goodwin via @amyhillman: "Slides and documents aren't the point: discussion and decisions are." For that reason, I've seen the wisdom of my provost's insistence on bringing together all the necessary people so that by the end of the discussion, a definitive decision can be made. On more than one occasion the provost has come looking for me on the spur of the moment to join her in a meeting, or to grab another of her colleagues out of existing meetings so that all the right people are there to make the necessary decision. As a result we've become a more decisive environment because we have the right discussions with the right people in real time. It's a simple and effective idea.

WHO'S ON THE TEAM?

> Difference drives deliciousness.

.

51

One of the lessons of the innovation literature is that a diversity of opinions and circumstances increases the likelihood of "happy accidents." A diverse group generates many conflicting possibilities, whereas a homogeneous group is likely to create a few agreeable ones. Thus, being able to choose members who represent a broad set of perspectives is key to arriving at the best possible outcome. I find myself listening a lot in meetings because I'm looking for the strongest ideas to emerge from the cacophony. Hearing the discussion has made me realize more than once that I hadn't accessed all the opinions possible to understand a situation, and it has convinced me to reverse a decision I'd thought I'd made. I've realized I wouldn't just be making an unpopular decision—I'd be making the *wrong* decision. So I listen when I can.

Discussing differences makes us feel uncomfortable, and it forces us to craft a path back to a new understanding. For example, in the classical frame of diversity, when I ran a committee at MIT focused on diversity issues, a student of Native American descent came to discuss how he felt discriminated against on multiple occasions. Trying to connect with this student, I related my own experiences of being called racial epithets at various points in my life owing to the color of my skin. I expected some degree of personal connection, but to my surprise he sharply responded, "You only experienced *immigrant* racism. I've experienced *indigenous* racism!" His comment gave me pause because I had never considered that these subtle shades of racism existed with varying degrees of discomfort ascribed. The student's perspective was so far afield from mine that I was forced to run a significant mental distance in a split second to respond, "You're right. Please tell me more."

> Misunderstanding is a missed opportunity to understand.
  When such opportunities are abundant, we all win.

Working in a group where there are considerable differences and disagreements can be a pain. When I was in my twenties I worked at a small foundation in Tokyo. There was one gentleman whom everyone disliked. I asked the director, a wise and esteemed scientist who cofounded one of the largest corporations in Japan, why he didn't just fire the guy. He gave me a quizzical look, as if that would be idiotic, and then replied, "Well, we need him, because an organization is like the human body. It needs viruses like him so the body can learn how to survive and remain strong." In a country that so appreciates conformity, it was surprising to hear him refer to the benefits of differences in an organization.

After that conversation, I began speaking with "the virus" more often and began to understand his unique value. He had a background in finance rather than the sciences like the rest of us. On more than one occasion, because he thought so differently, his point of view helped me avoid making errors in how I framed a problem. When he did not understand something, it became an opportunity to sort through our differences and construct a common frame built out of the misunderstanding. Learning is said to be most potent when "cognitive dissonance" occurs. Said more simply, we learn best when we are wrong.

> @johnmaeda likes what #RISD Provost Jessie Shefrin says about decision-
making, "It's not about top-down or bottom-up—it's about working together."

It's human nature: People at the top of the hierarchy naturally have a top-down bias; people at the bottom usually have a desire for more bottom-up decision-making authority. The late Gordon Mackenzie, in his dazzling book *Orbiting the Giant Hairball,* described this phenomenon as the difference between the pyramid and the plum tree. In the pyramid, the leader is way up on top so that she can see the entire horizon and most everyone else is way on the bottom, crushed by the oppressive weight of the pyramid. The plum tree inverts the pyramid, and the leader and her team are the roots at the bottom that feed resources into the tree. Employees are the leaves and plums at the very top that are nourished by the sun and have the best visibility to see how the work needs to get done. Mackenzie's healthy point is that leaders need to see themselves as community enablers more than community dictators.

> Alliances are grounded in reliances.

In my short time as president, I have already had moments when I felt the power and benefits of having a cohesive team. During the recent financial crisis, amid severe budget cuts, I chose to reduce my salary in an effort to "lead by example." My team immediately came forward and said, "We're not going to let you do that by yourself," and they unanimously chose to join in and cut their own salaries. I felt us all owning the responsibility of leadership together.

The image of teamwork that I always return to is a videogame screen that one of my former grad students, James Dai, showed me long ago. It depicted a bunch of people on the side of a mountain all connected to each other; the intent of the game was to teach kids that a team survives its way up the mountain because if any one person in the chain slips, the chain holds him up so that he does not fall. What is implicit in this analogy is that everyone on the team needs to bring her own set of strengths, because if one member consistently fails to deliver value, he jeopardizes the entire team's ability to make it to the top. Nobody signs on to be the weakest link in a chain; I've learned in building my own team that it's the ultimate responsibility of the leader to ensure that his team consists of the right members for the job at hand. It is the selecting, refining, and supporting the membership of that team that I now realize is well over 80 percent of my role.

Once after I spoke to one of my team member's staff meetings, I asked her to critique my performance, as I do with all of my colleagues. She systematically went through areas where I had done well and areas where I was lacking. My greatest deficiency was that I didn't deliver my message in a natural tone, the way she would have done more effortlessly than I with her staff. I knew she was right, and I told her that I was grateful to have her; because she was so strong at communicating with her staff, I didn't have to be.

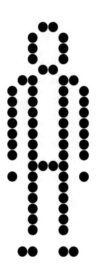

Human as Leader

They say that sometimes leadership is thrust upon you, and I now know that once it is, the responsibility and authority weigh heavily on your shoulders at all times. On one hand, the experience of leading is rewarding because you are in a position to positively enable others. On the other hand, leading often hurts, because the decisions you make can negatively affect a lot more people than just yourself. Being brought into an organization as an agent of change has been a humbling experience in balancing my dreams versus the realities presented, especially the realities presented in the economic climate I quickly encountered. I've discovered that your intention at the beginning always matters, and I try hard to remain true to the hopeful ideas that I brought with me, and to the ideals by which I guide myself. Knowing our limitations is what makes us human; ignoring them is what helps us believe we can lead.

INTEGRITY IS ALWAYS IN VOGUE

> Ideas lead to a result; ideals result in a leader.

I spoke at a conference in La Jolla in the 1990s and presented my then usual set of computational magic tricks involving flying computer graphics and exploding rectangles. After the presentation, I sat back down next to the much older speaker who had presented before me. During the applause for my talk, he leaned over to me and whispered, "Your work is so ... empty." A couple in the audience heard him say this and reassured me by kindly saying, "He's totally wrong. We love your work!" But I knew the man was right. At the time, living in a space of algorithms and abstract imagery, I felt an artistic detachment from all that was concrete. I was looking for what might replace the emptiness in my work with true substance and reality.

While at the Media Lab I was inspired by the work of former MIT president Jerome Weisner. He had worked as a young physicist during World War II on the so-called Manhattan Project that developed the nuclear bomb, and after the war he went on to devote the rest of his life to fostering world peace and integrating the arts into the sciences at MIT. I told this story to someone at a major electronics company who noted that there was a time in the world where all of the major laboratories were led by those who had experienced war firsthand. Because of its indelible effect on their lives, these people led with a rare kind of global conscience that he said has now largely evaporated from the leadership landscape. His comment helped me see the difference between *ideas* and *ideals*. Having ideals is having a compass that always points to your heart instead of your brain, and fulfillment isn't something you just imagine in your head but have to feel in your soul. In my own work I was free to express my ideas; as a leader I now strive to live up to my ideals.

> Doing right matters more than being right.

To care for the common good requires knowing what is good. Trouble is, what makes good leadership is a moving target. On the surface, working within the purity of technology and mathematical constructs has a kind of detached comfort. But even that work is values-laden. I realized this during one summer in my undergraduate years when I worked at a technology company developing pattern recognition software. I was given the assignment of finding patterns that looked like, of all things, tanks. Finding ways to compute a "right answer" to this problem was difficult but not impossible, and yet in the back of my mind there was the bigger question of whether engineering technologies to harm people was the right way to apply my skills. Many years later, I would use the same software development skills to create designs for companies and for my personal art projects that tended not to have a "right answer," but rather a "right feeling." Does helping companies sell their wares or creating objects that will disappear into private collections have any higher moral claim than creating military applications? I still don't know.

When I go on my morning jogs around campus, I listen to two of my favorite speeches by President Obama in a continuous loop—his famous "race speech" from the campaign trail, and his acceptance speech for the Nobel Prize. In the latter, he speaks about the importance of nonviolent means and diplomatic solutions to achieve resolution to conflicts. Yet at times, he says, meeting violence with violence can be the only way to resolve conflict. His message addresses the heavily nuanced line between just retaliation and unjust retaliation. The difference between the two is highly subjective and, again, has no single right answer.

I've been counseled by my board chair, Bank Rhode Island CEO and president Dr. Merrill Sherman, that if a leader ends any given day having done more than 50 percent good as opposed to bad, then she has had a day she can be proud of. I was puzzled by this at first, for when you think about the scale we're graded on throughout our lives (where over 90 percent is an A, 80 percent a B, and so forth), 50 percent is a failing grade. However, I now understand that the 50 percent refers not to the results you achieve on behalf of the institution—where a 90 percent-plus score should be the goal—but instead how your actions are perceived as "doing right" by others. It's often hard to get a read on how well you might be doing because the negative voices too often drown out the positive. But when people tell me—genuinely—that they support the work I am trying to do for the institution, it's always appreciated.

> A good ruler should use his straightedge if he starts going crooked.

I once had a boss who exhibited unethical and nasty behavior on a regular basis. Because a leader sets the tone for success, many in the organization emulated his behavior, thinking it would help them progress up the ladder. I've also had a boss who set the opposite example: As an executive, he was afforded a variety of perks that he often eschewed. Whether staying at a Holiday Inn instead of a more expensive hotel, or driving himself around in an old car instead of a chauffeur-driven company car, he exhibited a kind of unusual behavior applauded by many people—except of course for the other executives who felt pressured to reduce their own perks. Experiencing such examples of highs and lows in the workplace is the informal MBA education that everyone can acquire through observation. If people are lucky, they will have at least a few good bosses to guide their own behavior as they progress in life.

In my position as president of a college, certain entitlements are afforded to me. Things like a private car to drive me around (which I quickly gave up because it didn't suit me) or a presidential mansion (which I do have, but I choose to pay rent to the school and offer for others on campus to use) or something as small as a membership in a private dining club (which hasn't worked out for me and I've given up). In general, I try to adhere to the attitude that entitlement is the path furthest away from enlightenment—it's a belief that stems from my experience of becoming "suddenly" president which I don't want to forget. I believe many think of these perks as "deserved awards" for the hard work of being a leader, but I don't subscribe to that. During one of my open campus meetings during the financial crisis, a staff member asked everyone there to "think of a parent who is especially challenged paying a tuition bill" and how she might feel were she to review your expense statements. This is a simple guideline I now use every day.

> W+K's John Jay, "Find the truth. Then show why it matters."

A lot of the lessons I've learned about integrity have to do with what information to share and what not to share. As much as I have a bias toward transparency, sometimes I am faced with the fact that keeping some information confidential—like competitive secrets or details surrounding personnel matters—is the right road to take. In those cases, even explaining why you can't explain something is a valid way to get closer to the truth. For example, when I was asked in a large group why I couldn't speak about individual personnel matters in public, I underlined that if I were to share personal information publicly, like birth date, age, sexual preference, and so forth, then I not only would be entering legally suspect arenas, but also would be violating an individual's basic right to privacy. So when it is "the truth" that people seek, I've learned that sometimes the real truth lies in speaking to the principles that underlie why, in some cases, you, as the leader, must remain secretive. So always ask yourself, "What are the principles?" Say them to those who haven't yet heard them clearly, and start from there.

LEADING IN BETA

> Status quo can be a status symbol.

In taking on this position, I was given the awesome assignment by my board to build upon the enormous work of prior RISD presidents. In other words, to not only "not mess up" what was great about the country's pre-eminent art and design school, but to define the school's relationship with our new era of digital technology and global society. I found that my background signaled to many a possibility that I would put computers all over campus and replace all that was good about the legendary hand-crafted traditions of the school. But I didn't, and that's actually not my interest at all. In fact, I think of myself as someone who has become largely "technocritical" over these last ten years—as evidenced by the thinking in *The Laws of Simplicity* and grounded in the fact that I was raised by a traditional Japanese craftsman.

For an institution like RISD, which is on top of the heap, our status quo is actually something that competitors would die to have. In other words, sustaining the status quo in a nonleading institution is considered undesirable; in a leading institution the opposite is the case. What's being done right is being done by people who, in some cases, have been doing it right for a long time. So I know on the occasions when I've tried to suggest any radical changes to an existing process, the "it ain't broken so why fix it?" logic quickly rears its head. Worse, my suggestions can be taken as personal criticism directed not at the process but at the people doing the hard work.

The Hollywood movie *The Last Samurai* depicts the transition in late-1800s Japan from swords to guns as the winning means to wage war. The main protagonist, played by Tom Cruise, is an American who has been brought in to teach the Japanese how to use guns. By the end of the movie, he switches sides, finding greater beauty and honor in the samurai's ways of the sword. There is an allure to doing things the same way our forefathers did; it brings us closer to the birth of an idea or solution in its most pure form.

Preserving the honor and integrity of an original idea is a wonderful thing and is at the core of a prosperous, long-living institution. Many universities have existed for more than a century—longer than almost any other kind of organization—and it is this loyalty to the organization's core beliefs that is so integral to its longevity. For the institution that has already stood the test of time, the status quo has become a valid status symbol. And you can't blame anyone for trying to protect it with all their heart. Who wouldn't?

> When trust is broken, you have to start over from the beginning.
  Like muscle tissue, it can grow back stronger each time.

The financial crisis eroded credibility in leadership worldwide and for newer leaders like myself and, on a much larger scale, our nation's president, it was difficult to not pair the crisis with our own arrival. I felt a bit like Charlie Chaplin in the movie *Modern Times;* it was as if the machinery of the factory I had walked into on day one had pulled me onto the conveyor belt to get clobbered. I knew that RISD is the best possible fit for me—it offers me the opportunity to understand the power of art and design outside of the realm of technology—yet the timing worked out such that I had to learn quickly how to manage an institution through a difficult time and simultaneously calm a community that hadn't had a new leader in fifteen years. I felt like trust in me was being tested from the very beginning of my tenure as president.

These unexpected challenges brought to bear Harvard's Rosabeth Moss Kanter's famous saying, "the job makes the person." I am certainly a different person than when I originally started this journey. And that's the very reason I chose this experience; I had almost settled into the comfortable role of a senior tenured professor that would never require me to radically change. Yet as challenging as it was for me, it was even more challenging for my community, because they had to wrestle with the question of whether I was fit for the job. In the end, we all got through the world's financial heart attack together, and like all organizations out there we are recovering, rebuilding trust, and moving forward. It is a work in progress and truly still "in beta"—a phrase used in the software industry to describe a product that is "under construction" even after it has been released to the public.

CHANGE IS MANAGED BY CHANGE

> Rumors are like tumors.

So in a time of great change, I have had to make some changes. But the nature of the change undertaken has been different than I had expected from my original perspective as a professor—it is less about the intellectual questions and more about the operational aspects of my organization. Like other institutions that had to adjust their budgets given the sudden shift in our economy, I have had to preside over changes that directly and adversely affected the people in my community. And I realize that not an iota of "administrator-speak" can truly explain away the discomfort felt by people who have had to pick up the slack in organizations that have experienced reductions in personnel (not to mention those who unfortunately have lost their jobs).

I've observed firsthand how change and uncertainty create an informal stream of information—rumors—that quickly fills the unfilled vacuum of official information. Fueled by anonymous voices and emotional information that's extra-tasty (like junk food), these informal information structures situate themselves as the alternative locus of "the truth." In other words, rumors effectively transfer the power of spreading information away from the official structures—which tend to be slower, more methodical, and more measured—and toward informal structures that deliver "news" without any need to wait.

During my first year as president, I struggled to understand how rumors came to be, and how, given the damage they can cause, they could possibly be stamped out. I wanted to reclaim the power that the rumor mill generated as my own, and save the energy that people might waste speculating by expediently revealing all key facts and their rationales. I held many all-campus meetings during the battering of the economy to explain to the best of my ability what was happening to our institution financially. Yet if I were to do it all over again, I would have spent less time explaining and more time just listening. I realize now that rumors are a by-product of not only not knowing the facts, but also not feeling heard. Now that I'm taking time to have open office hours for staff and students along with faculty breakfasts, I know that these investments of time to truly

listen to what is being said has the potential to be like radiation therapy for any rumors, and I hope, to keep them in remission.

> Those who actively seek conflict as entertainment do so till they learn that front row is often directly on the stage.

Like many leaders in these rocky times, I have had moments when I felt like I was in the epicenter of directed conflict. It has caused me to think at length about the value of conflict and how it can be used productively. Constructive conflict is about building something, whether it's hatching a new idea through debate, or reaching a new goal through healthy competition between teams. Destructive conflict is about tearing things apart. A friend who owns a major manufacturing company in Brazil once expressed to me how important it is to acknowledge that the larger your company, the more likely your competition is not outside, but within. In a "red ocean" strategy of conventional warfare, the goal is to damage your competitors' boat so that the ocean turns red with your enemy's blood. But, he said, sometimes you need to look closely at the water because the blood is likely your very own—in other words, people on your boat are sabotaging each other. He explained that infighting and other team-breaking (versus team-building) behaviors can easily outweigh the damage inflicted by your competitors.

A faculty member once confronted me in a public forum and exclaimed that I was an outright liar; he went on to further express his dismay with my leadership. I responded that I used to be a professor like him, but had given up my academic freedom to become president. I now held a different job—to protect

his academic freedom to speak as he wishes to his president. After some time had passed, another professor privately shared his appreciation for my comments. He felt them to be consistent with what he taught his students about being skeptical of authority and questioning societal and organizational norms. It is by doing so that they will realize their future as innovators in art and design.

The line between respectful and disrespectful debate will inadvertently get crossed when situations are heated. I've begun to look more carefully at the nature of maintaining a respectful community, one that can retain the "good" skepticism of a learning environment, and at the same time self-regulate against destructive forces. That work is in the alpha stages, and some day I wish to report it when it goes into beta.

HUMILITY IS NOBLE

> Having a sufficiently big ego means you're comfortable enough not to have one at all.

I've had the fortune of knowing many people who are truly big deals in the fields of art, technology, design, business, or some combination thereof. They separate into roughly two categories: those with visible egos and those with invisible ones. Visibly egotistical people can't help but talk about themselves ad nauseam, but other stars seem so down to earth that you can easily mistake them for a waiter at an event. When I lived in Japan, I had the fortune of knowing Ikko Tanaka, one of Japan's greatest designers. He was the mind behind MUJI and other

significant Japanese brands in the seventies, eighties, and nineties. It seemed as if his work was in every museum collection in the world, and wherever he went, there was a red carpet rolled out for him.

One day he invited me to a dinner that he had prepared for his entire staff all by himself. At this dinner, he spent the whole time individually thanking each of his staff with food and kindhearted words. I was struck by this, as it was more typical to see staff being sent out to get cigarettes for such a Master, or being subjected to other demeaning kinds of displays of power and ego. When Mr. Tanaka passed away in 2002, I couldn't have been more thankful for the memory of his humility. He showed me that respect is constantly earned, and shouldn't be assumed because of your position.

The founder of the TED conferences, Richard Saul Wurman, has a simple rule of thumb for speakers on the stage: Be vulnerable. It sounds simple, but it's a departure for many of the highly accomplished people who serve as speakers there. Seeing others be vulnerable while standing on a stage, especially without the feigned protection of a lectern, allows the audience to be privy to something special: the speakers' humanity. That said, there's a fine line between vulnerability backed by confidence and seeming wimpy and spineless. Mr. Tanaka demonstrated the former better than anyone I've known to date.

> Saying you are sorry is meaningful only if your ego has left the room.

The Japanese have the word *sumimasen,* which simultaneously means "thank you" and "I'm sorry." It is an expression of gratitude for an act of kindness mated with asking for forgiveness for inconveniencing someone to deliver that kindness to you. Because Japan is such a tiny country and is so short on space, people are often caught physically close to each other, and inconveniencing each other is a regular occurrence. Saying "sorry" can also go beyond the simple *sumimasen.* You can add a bow for extra deference, or a deeper bow to go even one step further. So saying "sorry" is something of an art in that culture, and it requires special care.

Here in the United States, the rituals of apologizing may be less formal, but the act is no less important—or complex. A person came to meet with me after a heated public meeting where he was especially hostile toward me. He wanted to apologize for his behavior, and at the same time he made it clear that he did not want it to be known that he apologized. I was perplexed by this notion of a "private sorry." It carried some significance because of the personal effort made, but also it felt hollow in its execution because of his desire to keep it under wraps. I, in return, apologized back for putting him in a position to be angry in the first place. Then he responded that by apologizing to him, I had diminished the significance of his own apology.

I'm still working to get apologizing right in both cultures, because I believe in its power. I've witnessed that leaders rarely say "sorry," because they think it reduces their authority—it's seen instead as an admission of an error or, heaven forbid, a weakness that casts doubt on their leadership. As president, I find it tempting to believe that I am always right and to avoid the embarrassment of ever being wrong. Allowing that belief to consume you, however, makes you less human. Humans make mistakes. (Nature does, too, but it can't apologize; humans can.) I'm proud to follow the example of our country's president, who isn't afraid to apologize when he makes an error—just Google "Obama apologizes." President Obama gives us license as leaders to not always be right, but to instead always be real. Saying you're sorry can open a tightly closed door to another's heart. Saying you're sorry *for real* can open it wide and let possibility grow.

"thicker skin" x 75

Thank You

Thank you for staying to the end of this little book. It's essentially complete with the end of the last chapter, but there are a few tiny parting thoughts I wish to leave with you. Dissecting the experience of leading from the perspectives of an artist/designer, technologist, professor, and plain old human being has allowed me to gain confidence through learning as I go. If anything, I'm readying myself to learn even more from the experiences that lie ahead, and I remain open to the many criticisms that come with each accolade. For nothing can be worse than when my mentor, the late, great graphic designer Paul Rand, once said to me when I visited his home in Connecticut, "You ... may be ... THE ONE! *<long pause, and he looks away>* Naaaaaaaaah!" It pays to get dissed by the very best.

> Time may tick in seconds, but life is lived in years.

During an especially reflective year of my life, I wrote a simple program for the Web where you type in your age and it displays how many spring seasons you have left to live based upon the average life expectancy of your country.

You are: 43 years old living in [United States ▾]
(Springs Remaining) view by: ● group ○ line

❦❧ =77.1

It is a bit macabre, but it's also quite functional; it's like a progress bar that might appear on your computer while you are downloading a file—but for your life. I check on my "spring-counter," as it is called, from time to time, as it motivates me to live a life of welcoming seasons, thinking more clearly, seeing what counts, and forgetting more.

> @johnmaeda is thinking how positive acts often go unrewarded;
  negative acts always remain unforgotten. The choice is yours.

In general, I find the old adage "nice guys work harder" to be true. They usually choose to do the right thing even though it is usually less advantageous. For many years I worked with some-one at MIT who always chose the high road even when it did not serve him well personally. Whether by missing a meeting critical to his career advancement to instead tend to the needs of a student in trouble, or by defending a staff person who was being bullied by a higher-up, he operated without putting his own agenda first. In the end, when he left MIT, I was sorry to see such a good man go, and yet at the same time I was grateful to have had the opportunity to watch and learn from his rare, positive example. It never made complete rational sense but it always made superior ethical sense.

When a situation goes bad, there is often a desire to ascribe blame to a specific person or authority. And we all know the media especially love it when leaders go bad because such stories make for effective, sellable headlines. Pick any day and the negative outweighs the positive in the news. These stories validate our general skepticism about authority, and we feel reassured when those with high positions get brought back down to earth. Conversely, the positive actions of people like my friend so often go unnoticed.

> Momentum keeps the stopping away from the going.

One of my trustees periodically reminds me of a quote by the famous baseball hall-of-famer Casey Stengel: "The key to being a good manager is keeping the people who hate you away from those that are still undecided." Anyone with a dark sense of humor can't help but smile upon hearing this line. I've felt the power of achieving momentum with my team most recently with a slew of successes in fundraising for scholarships, greater sophistication in our recruitment efforts, and our efforts to link innovation with art and design in areas like, well, leadership. I feel that I've designed a winning team, which has been more work than any book, film, poster, computer program, lamp, or Web site I've ever designed. It's everything I wanted to do, and I had no idea how to do it. But the game's not over yet. We've only just started.

> Being grateful is knowing that "thank you" is not enough.

If you have something nice to say about a colleague, don't be embarrassed to say so. Acknowledgment is everything, and it's a rare skill that could seem to take too much time in a time-starved world. In this department I once again am inspired by my provost, Jessie Shefrin, who thoughtfully acknowledges those around her with personal telephone calls, hand-delivered flowers, written notes, or a pause for celebration during a meeting. I grew up in the famously "praise-free" world of MIT and of a traditional Japanese, Spartan-style upbringing, so this is something I watch and learn from Jessie. If she's reading this, I want her to know how much I truly thank her for her boundless support in our work together at RISD.

> The tide can sometimes turn in your favor. Rejoice when it happens.

Ending the week positively means that skill and luck worked in your favor. I'm always thankful when a weekend can serve as a space for reflection instead of a time for triage for one issue or another. I also try to remember to be grateful that e-mail traffic generally slows down after 6 pm. You can always count on it, so just wait for it diligently. And the sound of your heart—remember that it isn't a sound effect or some track set on repeat in your iPod's playlist. It's real, and it's working for you. So work for it a bit and get in some exercise today, and don't wait for tomorrow to break an honest sweat.

I am a firm believer that humor keeps us human. I know many of my tweets over these few years have been cryptically ironic, but that's usually a thinly veiled attempt to find what's comical in situations that often feel quite serious in the moment. It's my own personal form of therapy, of productively detaching and being reflective. The point of telling a joke isn't always to be funny—it can also be a way to get yourself to smile. And that feels good.

> Teaches chess to a child, "A king barely moves and has no power."
  Her reply, "The king is *most* powerful. If he dies, it's over."

I hope you got the sense from this book that I'm still learning how to lead, and I'm still trying to figure out what it means to be a leader. I'm inspired by the process of learning, and I thank all of you who have come along on the journey of this book, or my tweeting, to watch the process unfold. I think one of my biggest insights into my own growth as a leader occurred when I was teaching chess to one of my daughters. I showed her the zigzagging power of the bishop, the smooth motion of the rook, the diminutive one- or two-step dance of the pawn, and the hobbled singular steps of the king compared with the elegant omnipotence of the queen. "See the queen?" I said, "She's so powerful! But the king, he can only move one step at a time." It felt like how I feel myself as president sometimes. It has been humbling to realize how limited my moves feel as I get used to setting broad directions instead of getting the work done with my own (dirty) hands.

She looked at me quizzically in the way that seven-year-olds do, who see adults as all-knowing but sometimes frankly a bit off their rocker. Her simple reply was, "But daddy, the king is still powerful. Because if he dies, the game is over." I laughed when I realized how right she was, and how the impact of a leader comes from more than the individual moves he makes. The leader makes sure his organization is operating fairly, joyfully, for the right cause, and with gratitude. And he makes sure that thanks are constantly given to all those who have chosen to join the team. I hope you can apply some of the learnings from my journey thus far, for the world is in need of people to participate in leading its transformation. Perhaps, as Rand said to me, "You ... may be ... THE ONE!" Thanks for coming, and good luck.

Visit redesigningleadership.com to continue the journey.

Acknowledgments

We'd like to thank the many folks at MIT Press who believed in this little book—especially Robert Prior and Ellen Faran for their pioneering belief in simplicity.

Thank you to our families for their support and feedback: on Becky's side Don, Jane, Alex, and Chloe, and to my wife Kris and our daughters Mika, Rie, Saaya, Naoko, and Reina.

Thank you to RISD's Board of Trustees for giving me the opportunity to take a creative approach to the college presidency. Board Chair Merrill Sherman once described my appointment in two words: "calculated risk." I sincerely hope that her calculations turn out to be correct (smile). Special thanks to Robert DiMuccio, Stephen Key, Dick Haining, and Duncan Johnson for their mentorship, and to Erica DiBona for all her moral support—and for the cookies too!

Thank you to all who provided input along the way, including Jaime Marland and Albert Lee. And thank you to Marina Mihalakis and Mara Hermano for the kind of support that every president dreams about, but I get to live every day.

Thank you to my executive leadership team at RISD, which includes Becky, for being an agile, collaborative, and hopeful group of people who have shown me how to lead—which is, simply, to be lucky enough to lead a great team.

Last, and most important, thank you to the faculty and staff of RISD, and to all of RISD's students and graduates, for all that you imagine and *do* that helps the world experience the importance of art and design in this new century. It is RISD's time.